ARRIVA THE SHIRES

THE LAST TWENTY-FIVE YEARS

GARY SEAMARKS

AMBERLEY

First published 2026

Amberley Publishing
The Hill, Stroud
Gloucestershire, GL5 4EP

www.amberley-books.com

British Library Cataloguing in Publication Data.
A catalogue record for this book is available from the British Library.

ISBN 978 1 3981 2853 8 (print)
ISBN 978 1 3981 2854 5 (ebook)

Typeset in 11pt on 14pt Sabon.
Typeset by Simon and Sons ITES Services Pvt. Ltd., Chennai, India.
Printed in Great Britain.

Appointed GPSR EU Representative:
Easy Access System Europe Oü, 16879218
Address: Mustamäe tee 50, 10621, Tallinn, Estonia
Contact Details: gpsr.requests@easproject.com,
+358 40 500 3575

Acknowledgments

Thanks for help on this book, either directly or indirectly, are extended to David Beddall, Matt Robinson for help filling gaps in my vehicle histories; as usual the PSV Circle for its constant supply of info over the past forty years, and nowadays various online sources with news and tip-offs before it happens it seems; also my wife Helen for spending many hours in retail outlets while I obtain that missing image; and lastly all those who have purchased this publication.

Introduction

2026 marks forty years since United Counties was divided into three separate companies, United Counties based in Northampton covering Northants, North Bedfordshire and Huntingdon, Milton Keynes CityBus based within the then new town and Luton & District, covering South Bedfordshire, North Hertfordshire and South Buckinghamshire.

This book follows on from my earlier *Luton and District to Arriva the Shires* publication, and is my potted history between 2000 and 2025, covering the vehicles operated under the Arriva the Shires licence in that period. The core operating area of South Bedfordshire, Hertfordshire and Buckinghamshire is focused on, with boundary changes occurring with other Arriva operations across in East Herts and Essex that are outside the scope of this edition.

Three major acquisitions had occurred in the early part of the twenty-first century with firstly in late 2000 Oxford Bus Company, part of the Go-Ahead Group, selling its High Wycombe garage and services to The Shires, along with about fifty mostly elderly vehicles. Early 2005 would see the remaining part of the Sovereign business centered on Stevenage acquired, including the Green Line 797 and 798 routes into London Victoria. Then in 2006 Arriva bought MKMetro at Milton Keynes, which had been part of United Counties until 1986, after which it had passed through several owners, including Stagecoach for a short while, when acquired as part of the Cambus operation in 1996. In all this added a total of about 200 vehicles to the fleet strength. While the High Wycombe and Stevenage acquisitions were rebranded into Arriva the Milton Keynes operation retained the MKMetro name until 2010, with vehicles not transferring to The Shires operating licence until 2013, although vehicles cascaded into the fleet remained in Arriva livery.

Three Green Line routes were operated into Central London, with the frequent 757 from Luton and its airport. Hemel Hempstead ran the 758 and Stevenage the 797 and 798, in addition to which several longer-distance services were operated between larger urban centres, with High Wycombe reaching Reading and Aylesbury going to Oxford. While the Green Line routes used coaches, several other of the long-distance routes ran under the Sapphire and Max brands with the added bonus of free Wi-Fi and better seating fitted. The growth of Luton Airport saw the 757 service gaining custom, which was also helped by online marketing and joint ticketing with EasyBus, Megabus, Terravision and National Express. A batch of tri-axle Van Hools arrived in 2008 for the service, but in 2013 Luton Airport went into partnership giving National Express access rights to the airport bus station and not Green Line. For a while a shuttle bus was provided to a remote car park for onward transfer to the 757 but later things were sorted out and the service returned to the airport.

In 2013 the Luton–Dunstable Guided Busway opened along part of the former long-closed railway line to Leighton Buzzard; Arriva were one of three operators to provide high-frequency fast services along the track. South of the town a short section of reserved unguided bus-only road has cut times between the town and airport.

Management changes were implemented in 2016 that were to see the company in effect split up, with Stevenage and Hemel Hempstead passing into the control of Arriva Kent Thameside along with the East Herts and Southend operations. Garston (Watford) would move to Arriva London North for its Transport for London services, while its local services would be based at Hemel Hempstead Garage. Garston Garage would close in 2018 due to high running costs, while the remaining garages of Luton, Milton Keynes, Aylesbury and High Wycombe would remain on The Shires licence, but the legal address would move from Dunstable Road, Luton, to Arriva Midlands' Leicester address.

Operation of the Green Line 758 had transferred from Hemel to Luton Garages in 2018 including a small batch of Van Hool coaches, but by late 2020 the service was withdrawn. Like all operators, things took a downward turn during and after Covid-19 when buses were devoid of passengers and revenue. Between August 2017 and August 2024 the only new vehicles were the fourteen Busway Volvo B8RLE for Luton and twenty-two coaches for the 757, of which six have been moved on.

2024 would see the company withdraw its operations from South Buckinghamshire with both High Wycombe and Aylesbury depots closing in July, some services of the latter transferring to other depots, but many other routes were replaced by other operators. Ironically many High Wycombe services were picked up by Carousel Buses, who were owned by Go-Ahead, which had sold out to Arriva in the town twenty-four years earlier. While services at Aylesbury were picked up by local independents, leaving The Shires sphere of operation based around Luton/Dunstable and Milton Keynes and several inter-urban routes. June 2025 would also see the end of Arriva on the Town services in Leighton Buzzard, just two years after a new network had been introduced in conjunction with the local council that included evening and Sunday services for the first time. A new operator was brought in to run the replacement slimmed down network.

A major investment in new rolling stock occurred in the second quarter of 2025, with thirty new Volvo B8RLE MCV Evora buses arriving for Luton, for a major recast of Busway services, which included routes to new developments to the north of Luton and Dunstable. Vehicles displaced included similar thirty-eight-seat ones that moved on to work in Merseyside.

Many differing types of vehicles have been used by the fleet in the past twenty-five years. With the former Arriva dealership being DAF dealers, it is not surprising that they formed a major part of the intake, alongside Volvo, Scania, Optare, Mercedes and ADL products. Wright bodywork had been a long-term choice so it's not surprising that the Streetlite has also featured, with single decks in the WF and DF (wheels first and doors first) options. A batch of Electric WF models were taken for an extended test period in Milton Keynes in late 2014 and retired in 2019. One of the biggest changes in the fleet has been the move away from double deckers, with only twenty-five new ones entering service outside the TfL contracts between 2001 and 2024, most of which were for the now withdrawn Aylesbury–Oxford route. Cascades of vehicles have been transferred both into and out of the fleet from the Midlands and Midlands North operation, some short term while others have remained until disposal out of the group.

Gary Seamarks
Bedfordshire

The first new double-deckers for Luton & District had been a batch of twelve Leyland Olympians with Alexander RL bodywork delivered in late 1988. 636 (F636 LMJ) was one of a pair that were fitted with high back seats for use on private hire as and when needed. During the 1997 renumbering it became 5086 and would last until 2011. In this 2010 image at Luton it is running the staff shuttle.

New to Aylesbury as 647, G647 UPP was one of the second batch of Olympians with Alexander RL bodies with Luton & District, as 5097, seen in July 2011 on a market day in Leighton Buzzard working a town route to Meadow Way. The passage of buses behind the stalls was always of concern. All buses were later removed from the High Street to nearby West Street on market days.

Carrying extensive in-house advertising for driver recruitment in 2008 was 5141 (N41 JPP), a Northern Counties-bodied Volvo Olympian which had been new to Luton, but later moved across to Aylesbury from where it's seen operating the frequent service to Oxford railway station, via the city centre.

Early 1991 saw the arrival of G131 YWC, a long wheelbase Leyland Olympian with eight-three-seat Northern Counties body from Ensignbus. It would be allocated to High Wycombe as LRL 31, becoming 5134 in 1997. Eleven years later it's seen in its home town.

Fifteen Volvo Olympians with Northern Counties Palatine II bodies arrived new in the summer of 1998, with 5146–54 allocated to Watford and 5156–61 to Aylesbury. They seated sixty-eight and were amongst the first vehicles in the new Arriva livery in the fleet. 5151 (S151 KNK) is seen in High Wycombe in July 2008.

Branded as line 280, which linked Aylesbury, Thame, Wheatley and Oxford, is Volvo Olympian 5159 (S159 KNK). As can be seen the batch of fifteen were fitted with high-backed seating in their Northern Counties Palatine II bodies with reduced capacity to thirty-nine over twenty-nine. These would be the last step entrance buses purchased new.

Above and below: Acquired with the London Country North West fleet in October 1990 were fifteen Leyland-bodied Olympians for use on tendered London route 142 between Watford Junction and Brent Cross, with seven more arriving in 1991. As new rolling stock arrived so these were cascaded to other locations. 5120 (G290 UMJ) is seen in High Wycombe during the summer of 2008, while 5117 (G287 UMJ) was allocated to Milton Keynes when seen in 2009. Due to the full-height bodies they were restricted to selected garages.

Also seen at Wycombe is 5836 (WLT 916), which had started life with London Buses in March 1986 as L16 (C816 BYY), fitted with an ECW body that was originally dual doored, being converted to single door in 2006 shortly after arriving from Arriva East Herts & Essex. After being withdrawn, it was sold to Ensign and later operated by two independents in Buckinghamshire.

With the purchase of Wycombe Bus in December 2000 an additional fourteen Leyland Olympians were added to the fleet, including 5831 (G231 VML) with Alexander RL bodywork, which by 2009 had been transferred to Luton, where it is seen on a crew shuttle bus, again having been new as dual doored and later rebuilt.

The first low-floor double-deckers to arrive in the fleet were a batch of twelve ALX400-bodied Dennis Tridents in the summer of 2000 for Luton. 5421 (W421 XKX), numerically the first of the batch, had moved across to Aylesbury in early 2006 and is captured in Milton Keynes a few weeks later.

Alongside the twelve Tridents allocated to Luton, a further fifteen similar vehicles were placed in service at Southend depot of Arriva East Herts and Essex, including 5443 (W443 XKX), which by 2012 had become part of the Luton allocation and is seen here in Silver Street on a local route in February 2012.

Above and below: Two Showbus shots of 5425 (W425 XKX), firstly at Duxford in 2012, while at Ware depot promoting the 'plusbus' ticketing that had recently been introduced in many locations. Then in 2019 with its Love Luton livery. By this time it was mainly used on school duties, lasting until the spring of 2024 and the demise of the type in the fleet.

Although route branded for the 500 Aylesbury–Watford service, Alexander-bodied Trident 5422 (W422 XKX) is seen leaving Oxford on the 280 back to Aylesbury via Thame in 2011. When new this bus was one of a batch of twelve allocated to Luton.

Located to the north of the town centre, Barnfield College is one of the main centres of higher education in the Luton area. 5432 (W432 XKX) was wrapped in this livery for its latter years and used on routes passing the site. When new the seating on the upper deck was configured for fifty-one but down seated to a more comfortable forty-seven before entry to service.

Taken in Oxford in 2008, 5431 (W431 XKX) is a few minutes into its return trip to Aylesbury via Thame on the 280. As an overall advert for Aylesbury based Mix96, 5431 was one of the batch new to Luton for use on the busy 38 route to Dunstable via Houghton Regis.

Seen in the now closed Hemel Hempstead bus station when only a few months old, 5455 (SN58 EOB) is about to head out on its branded route for a trip to Maple Cross via Watford and Rickmansworth. The highbacked seating is evident in this image.

Like many businesses Arriva were suffering a shortage of drivers post Brexit and Covid. 5460 (YY14 WFU) is seen here in Oxford, with in-house advertising for its driver recruitment, starting a quieter mid-morning run back across the Chilterns in June 2021.

Aylesbury based 5464 (SN15 LPP) is seen on Rail Replacement work at Luton on bank holiday Monday in May 2021, working a Thameslink service to Bedford. Much of the Luton Interchange site is located on the site of the former Luton Bute Street railway station that was closed in 1966, which was served by trains on the line from Hatfield to Leighton Buzzard that connected Luton and Dunstable on its way.

Transfers from Arriva Midlands in 2021 saw the arrival of 4400/1 (YY14 LHD/E) at Aylesbury for use on the 280. The former is seen in Thame in September 2021 still with route branding for its former route in Derby. They would later move across to Milton Keynes when the 150 route was moved there, before returning to the Midlands operation.

Early 2025 brought a batch of Enviro400s into Milton Keynes from Leicester where they had been displaced by new electric buses. This in turn allowed the Volvo B9TLs to be cascaded to Luton to allow the Transbus-bodied Volvo B7TLs to be withdrawn. Here 4435 (CX58 GBV) sets out at the start of an X4 to Aylesbury where the extra capacity of double deckers is handy around school times.

East Lancs Lowlander-bodied DAF DB250 6061 (FD02 UKP) loads at MK Shops for an early evening run back to Aylesbury via Leighton Buzzard, on a timing that would have been a limited stop run to High Wycombe in NBC days ran by Alder Valley as part of the X15, which ran between Northampton and Reading, but mostly consisted of part route services except on Sundays.

Luton has always had a need for low-height double deckers due to a couple of bridges on the Midland Main line near Leagrave station. Cascaded in during 2016 were a batch of East Lancs Lowlander-bodied DAF DB250. 4714 (FE51 YWM) is seen departing Dunstable on a wet spring Saturday morning in 2018 on a 31 to Luton.

The single-door conversion can be picked out on 6283 (Y483 UGC), an ALX400-bodied DAF DB250 that arrived in the fleet in March 2013, having been new to Arriva London as DLA 283, where it lasted for thirteen years and would see another six years' service before sale to Hardwick as scrap.

Leaving Aston Clinton towards Aylesbury is VDL DB250 Wright Pulsar Gemini 6047 (LJ04 LGV), which had been new to Arriva London as DW77, looking devoid of passengers as the bus in front was running late and had only passed through a couple of minutes earlier. The 500 route would pass to Hemel Hempstead upon the closure of Aylesbury, but would be withdrawn completely within twelve months.

Above and below: Cascaded into Aylesbury during 2017/8 were a batch of eleven Volvo B7TLs from Midlands at Leicester, which had been new to the London North fleet in the autumn of 2001 as dual-doored vehicles. For their life after London all were converted to single-door layout and reregistered to disguise their age. 4015 (UUI 2944) was new as LF51 DFL, while 4018 (LF51 DFU) became UUI 2910. Because the Gemini Eclipse bodies were full height, they were restricted in which garages they could operate from. Both are seen in Aylesbury in the twilight of their careers, with the final one leaving the fleet in 2022.

Cascades from the Medway towns in 2023 brought a handful of Transbus ALX400-bodied Volvo B7TLs into Luton to help remove older Tridents with similar bodywork. 6439 (GN04 UFH) is seen working a 24 service in October 2023. The batch were replaced within a couple of years by more cascaded vehicles.

Seen in High Wycombe in the final couple of weeks that Arriva were operating in the town is 6144 (FJ56 OBE), a former Arriva Midlands Volvo B7TL with Wright Eclipse Gemini bodywork. Although lacking a blind, it was still looking smart after sixteen years' service.

The sole Volvo B9TL at Milton Keynes in early 2025 was 4201 (FJ08 LVM), which arrived in having been new to Arriva Midlands North at Tamworth for its CityLynx service into Birmingham before transferring to Leicester. As can be seen it still retained an older Arriva livery when captured in Milton Keynes on an X6 to Aylesbury.

New to Derby in 2008, Volvo B9TL 4210 (FJ58 KXH) was one of several Wright Eclipse Gemini double deckers that were transferred into Milton Keynes during the spring of 2020 to allow for additional passengers while social distancing was in force. July 2020 sees it working the busy 3 route that served both Coachway and a large industrial and warehouse park.

Above and below: Cascaded down from Yorkshire in 2024 were a batch of eleven Volvo B9TLs with Optare Olympus eighty-one-seat bodywork. The batch were split between Milton Keynes and Luton initially, although unfortunately one of the Luton batch would be claimed by the low bridge at the station shortly after arrival. 4106 (YJ08 EEG) is seen in Stony Stratford, while 4114 (YJ08 EEU) is seen in Luton where all the batch are now based.

Former Arriva North West 4436 (CX58 GBY) was one of a batch of nine ADL Enviro E400s that arrived in Milton Keynes in early 2025, where they replaced the Optare Olympus Volvo B9TLs that were cascaded to Luton. They were put to use on the busy 5/6 cross-city route and the X4 and X6 to Aylesbury, as can be seen. 4436 retains the Pride Rainbow.

One of the former Arriva Yorkshire Optare Olympus-bodied Volvo B9TLs 4115 (YJ08 EEV) arrived in Luton complete with its Pride Rainbow. It's seen here working the 1 route, which in old money is the former 31 route direct to Dunstable, but now runs a loop round the Farley Hill Estate in Luton then back to Dunstable. It has been many years since double deckers served the Farley Hill part of town.

Upgrading of the TfL contracts in 2002 saw the arrival of twenty-five DAF DB250 with Alexander ALX400 bodies at Watford. These were all painted in TfL red unlike the vehicles they replaced and were also step-free access and dual doored. 6003 (KL52 CWR) is almost ten when seen at Edgware, working a 340 to South Harrow, which the company ran between 1991 and 2018.

Half of the first batch of Alexander ALX400-bodied DAF DB250s was cascaded off TfL work to other depots from late 2012, repainted into aquamarine and converted to single door layout with additional seating. First of the batch 6000 (KL52 CWN) has just arrived at Milton Keynes in this 2015 shot. It would last with the company until 2021 before its fate was sealed when sold to a dealer for scrap.

3260 (V260 HBH) was a Volvo B6LE with Wright Crusader 2 bodywork that arrived in late 1999. Only three of the type were purchased new by the company, 3258–60. This one's working life was ended in 2015 with fire damage. By the demise of Garston (Watford) Garage in 2018 a lot of its work was under contract to Transport for London, which specified its standard livery be applied.

A second batch of eleven DAF DB250s would arrive in 2006 for TfL work. These would be fitted with the Wright Pulsar Gemini bodywork. Numbered 6026–36 by The Shires, they would later become DW135–45 with Arriva London North. 6027 (YJ55 WOA) is seen at Watford Junction when about to be taken back to the garage in this 2012 shot.

Seen at Edgware bus station in 2012 is 3218 (S315 JUA), a Dart SLF that had been new to Arriva London North and acquired in late 2008, and would last until 2014 before sale as scrap. The 305 route was operated for TfL between 2006 and 2018.

New to Arriva London South was Dart SLF Plaxton Pointer 3223 (S306 JUA) arriving at Watford in early 2010. It was repainted into Aquamarine and deployed on non-TfL work, as seen here in 2012 in its home town, followed by 6024.

3719 (YE06 HPF) was one of a batch of twenty DAF SB120s with Wrightbus Cadet 2 bodywork purchased for TfL work in 2006. Having been renumbered to DWL88 in 2016 with the intention of being transferred with others to control of Arriva London North when they took over Watford Garage later that year, because of fire damage the transfer never happened, with the inevitable sale to a breaker instead.

Edgware bus station again is the location for this shot of 3805 (SN56 AXH) that had been new in late 2006 to Wycombe garage for the U9 route at Uxbridge. By 2008 it had moved across to Watford where it would remain until the garage transferred to Arriva London North control in late 2013, becoming PDL151 in the process.

Above and below: Thameslink's new timetable for May 2018 saw services fall well below expectations, with standby buses soon located to various key stations to help solve any problems. PDL122 (LJ05 GPO) was one of several Darts moved up from London to help. It's seen here in late June at Luton, while Scania 3608 (KE55 GVY) is seen at Bedford the following month with PDL117 (LJ05 GOP) and another awaiting a possible call.

Above and below: Another rail replacement contract operated was for London Northwestern, between Bletchley and Bedford. Milton Keynes-based 3126 (YX17 NPK) is seen in May 2020 heading towards Bletchley at Stewartby, while Aylesbury's Citaro 3018 (BD12 DJE) awaits time at the same location with the first service of the day to Bletchley in August 2021. Due to limited access at several of the smaller stations a minibus service was also operated, with the big buses operating limited stop.

With its passenger carrying life over Plaxton Pointer-bodied Dart K407 FHJ passed to Luton Council for use as a welfare bus at night. It's parked on Manchester Street at roughly the site of the 1970s town bus station.

Watford Junction station was the long-term home of 3361 (K411 FHJ), a former East Herts Dennis Dart with Plaxton Pointer bodywork that had been converted into a driver's restroom. Back in 2012 Watford Garage had TfL routes that terminated at the station.

Six MAN 14.220 with MCV bodies were transferred in during 2013/14 to High Wycombe from the Telling's Golden Miller operation. 3747 (AE56 MDV) would later become one of several that were converted to trainers carrying what was quite an attractive version of the Arriva 2017 livery, and renumbered 9558, as seen in April 2018 on Midsummer Boulevard in Milton Keynes where it was based before being scrapped in 2021.

Captured at the Showbus 2022 is Trainer T62 (LJ08 CXS), a former Arriva London E400 now relegated to driver training duties outside the capital, that was several years younger than the Tridents still in use at the time.

Several of the garages had relocated out of the town centres in recent years including Luton in 2001 to a more remote Dunstable Road location, meaning that additional staff transfers were required. This 2016 image at Luton Interchange shows two of a batch of former London Taxis with in-house advertising that were bought for the purpose.

Milton Keynes garage is another that needs a ferry bus operation for staff at the start and finish of some shifts. This August 2018 shot shows Renault YX08 FWD on Midsummer Boulevard. Its days were by then numbered as it left the fleet the following month.

Above and below: Between 1995 and 1998 a total of eighty-six Mercedes Minibuses with Plaxton Beaver bodywork were purchased new spread across most garages. 2133 (N913 ETM) had been new as MP263 prior to the renumbering and allocated to Watford, but later transferred to Luton where it's seen in 2009 working a town service. Meanwhile, 2185 (R185 DNM) carries the restyled Beaver 2 bodywork, which was slightly longer. It's seen on a Stevenage Town route in 2008.

The company secured several contracts with Bucks County Council, which would see the introduction of six twenty-three-seat 8.5-metre Optare Solos at Aylesbury in April 2001 on lease from the council, including 0442 (Y42 HBT). All carried the Bucks County Council-inspired livery.

The final Optare Solos to be taken new were 2508–10 for MKMetro in late 2009, with 2510 (YJ09 OTZ) seen in Milton Keynes when almost new starting a journey on the tendered 33 to Northampton via the villages.

Optare had restyled the Solo and launched the SR model. 2509 (YJ58 CCK) is an M890SL model which had been new to Arriva Derby in 2008, but ten years later was allocated to High Wycombe garage. It remained the only one of this model operated.

Solo 0441 (YJ10 LZV) had been purchased to provide a service to the new Sandhills residential development of Leighton Buzzard in 2010. With suitable branding, it's seen in June 2012, and would later be painted in an all-over orange for the route, both branded as Dash D1.

The Loop service was introduced in early 2025 operating a fixed service that covered areas that had previously had tendered services removed, then replaced with a DRT scheme. 2408 (YJ58 VCG) was one of two Solos branded up for the service in the first few months, providing a roughly hourly service in either direction, the full loop taking almost two hours to complete.

Several of the Mercedes City45 with EVM have been cascaded into the fleet over the past few years. 1002 (BF67 WGP) arrived in 2019 from Midlands North to Aylesbury, where it is seen in July 2021 on the now withdrawn town route 9 to Stoke Mandeville. At this time it seemed that any type of bus was used on the route, which became Aylesbury depot's last town service.

1129 (RX18 LNG) was another cascaded Mercedes City45, this time from the Arriva Cymru fleet. Its main usage at Milton Keynes has been as a staff shuttle bus, with little clue that it is an Arriva vehicle to the untrained eye.

Looking more like some kind of delivery van, this Mercedes City45, 1020 (BF67 WGW), was in fact an advert bus for the Hemel Storm Basketball team, seen here in Luton in April 2024, having been transferred across from Hemel Hempstead.

Ten Optare Versas were taken new into the fleet. All were allocated to Watford in January 2013, numbered 3413–22. They were transferred to the Arriva Kent Thameside operation with the Hertfordshire operations. KX62 JJO, new as 3413, is seen in Hertford in 2023 now numbered 4185 by its new owners.

Versa 2991 (YJ09 MKE) was an unusual allocation to Luton during 2020, when it was on a short-term visit to the fleet from the Arriva Midlands fleet. It's captured here at the town's Interchange, with a Grant Palmer Solo for company and a Thameslink Class 700 unit awaiting departure in the station.

To capture the Opare Versa within the fleet would mean a trip to High Wycombe during the latter life of the batch. 2952 (YJ61 MHU) leaves the town's bus station on a local trip to Micklefield during the last few weeks of Arriva's presence in the Buckinghamshire town, having been transferred in from Arriva Midlands as part of a batch to update the depot in early 2023.

A very wet High Wycombe sees 2401 (YJ57 EKF), one of a pair with 2402 of Optare Versa V1100 that had arrived new the previous autumn in this all-over orange route branding. The framework in place for the new Sainsbury's store can be seen in the background.

Above and below: Wrights Streetlite with Door First option (DF) first appeared in the fleet in mid-2014, when 3651–60 took to the road from Watford Garage. Branded as Sapphire, they were put to work on the busy inter-urban 321 route via St Albans to Luton. 3654 (LK14 FTD) heads through Watford Junction in early 2023 at a period when the route had been extended west to Maple Cross, while 3655 (LK14 FTE) is seen in Church Street, Luton, in 2016 heading for the Interchange, in its original livery. The batch of ten were transferred with the operation of the 321 to Luton in May 2016, after which they were found often on local work.

Above and below: To remove older vehicles a cascade of Streetlite DF was implemented from Midlands with around two dozen arriving. The bulk were for Milton Keynes, but 3301/2 (FJ64 EVB/C) were for use at Luton. The latter is seen at Luton Interchange again on the 321 in 2017, while 3340 (FJ64 JYL) is seen on layover at Milton Keynes station. Construction work starts on Unity Place, which would change this backdrop.

Former Arriva Kent Thameside 4278 (GN14 DXW) arrived at Luton in July 2022, and was numbered 2310 in the fleet, to take the place of 3658, which had been written off in an accident a few weeks earlier. It is seen on Silver Street with The Mall shopping centre behind.

Carrying the Connect Hertfordshire advertising is Wright Streetlite DF 3652 (LK14 FTA), one of two with this scheme applied, although often on the 321 across to Watford via St Albans. On this day more mundane work would see it staying around the town.

Above and below: Two batches of Wrights Diesel Streetlite WF (Wheel First) were taken in 2015, which were split between Luton, 2511–24, and High Wycombe, 2525–8. All arrived in a blue and green livery as seen by 2511 (LM64 JNV), which had moved to Milton Keynes by 2018, which promoted the green credentials of these thirty seaters. They were renumbered in 2018 to 2311–28. By the time of repaints they would reappear in standard Arriva livery as seen here of 2326 (LK15 FFU) at High Wycombe in 2024.

Eight battery-powered Wright Streetlite WFs were placed in service in Milton Keynes in late 2013 on route 7 between Bletchley, CMK and Wolverton as part of a trial. They were finished in a non-standard livery as shown by 5004 (KP63 TDZ) passing The Point in early 2015.

2303 (KP63 TDX) is seen at Bletchley bus station in the summer of 2018 after the batch had been renumbered from 5001–8 to 2301–8. The large plate between the axles is a ground contacting charger used at terminal points to boost the batteries of the vehicle. One down point was that it extended the layover times of the route.

Wright loaned DRZ 9713 Streetlite to the company in 2019. Its Northern Ireland plates hide the fact that it was new in February 2012, and had been used across the UK as a demonstration vehicle in its early life. Here it's filling in for absent Streetlite 3654 that was sent to Germany with gearbox faults.

Reliability issues with the electrics saw two diesel-powered sisters arrive in 2014 from Wrightbus in this silver livery. Both had been demonstrators beforehand. 449 (HRZ 6499) is seen in 2020 at Milton Keynes station towards the end of its stay in the fleet, and after the electric trial had been concluded.

One of a pair of Plaxton Primas that arrived into Luton in April 2013 from Telling Golden Miller is 2600 (LF08 DZW). They were both initially used on a feeder service from Luton Airport to an off-airport car park when the airport would not allow the 757 access, due to commercial reasons. After it was sorted, the pair were moved across to Stevenage.

During the spring of 2023 a new revised network was implemented in Leighton Buzzard, with funding provided that allowed all routes within the town boundary to be run without charging fares until Christmas. Five almost new AD E20D vehicles, including 3154 (YX72 OFL), were transferred from Kent for the network at the same time Milton Keynes assumed control for maintenance of them, with four being required to maintain the town services and the fifth spare. However, a change of operator on contract renewal in June 2025 saw Arriva no longer the operator of these services.

Between 1999 and early 2000 a batch of around thirty Dart SLFs with twenty-nine-seat Plaxton Pointer bodies were introduced as part of a fleet upgrade. 3288 (V288 HBH) was typical of the batch. They were allocated to most depots and helped replace step entrance older minibuses. The route 4 and its partner route 1 ran to the Farley Hill Estate in Luton with a thirty-minute round trip.

The town operation in Leighton Buzzard was a mix of smaller buses and deckers for many years. Transbus Dart Pointer MPD 3839 (KE53 NFC) had been new to High Wycombe, for use on a Transport for London contract at Uxbridge, but in 2018 it was in the second Arriva livery and in use at Leighton Buzzard.

New to Hemel Hempstead in 1999 was 3229 (T829 NMJ), one of a batch of 10.7-metre Dennis Darts with Plaxton Pointer bodies that seated thirty-nine, seen here in loading for Watford in 2009 in the original Arriva provincial livery of aquamarine and Cotswold stone.

Delivered new to Hitchin, Dart SLF Pointer 3497 (W497 YGS) had been cascaded across to Aylesbury by 2008 and painted in a red version of the Arriva livery for use on the 9 route to Stoke Mandeville. Perhaps the use of red would not be the best choice with the arrival in town of Red Rose, Red Eagle and Redline. In September 2023 Arriva would no longer operate any town routes in Aylesbury.

Luton's 2211 (SN03 LGE) was also a cascade from the Midlands, arriving in the second half of 2017. It's seen here in Luton in 2021 in what perhaps could be described as a unique version of an Arriva livery, but perhaps shows how robust these old Darts are.

Having been new to Arriva London as PDL60, Plaxton Pointer MPD Dart 2159 (LJ51 DCF) would spend its last three years in service at High Wycombe, finally being withdrawn in 2021 just short of twenty years. Unlike many ex-TfL vehicles, this 8.8-metre example was also single doored.

Cascades between Arriva Midlands see plenty of midlife plus movements into High Wycombe, with 2297 (BF52 NZP) being no exception when it arrived in April 2017. It's seen here some eighteen months later looking in need of some TLC on a town route, and would be sold out of the fleet in 2021.

Watford Junction station is the where we find 3502 (KE51 PTU) in May 2012, new in October 2001 to Watford, it was one of the first vehicles in the fleet to carry the new registration system. Four in the batch 3500–2/9 were initially for TfL route 350 between Watford and South Harrow, but were later used on other TfL routes, before repaint into the provincial livery.

Working route SB8 in Stevenage in June 2008 was 3416 (P416 HVX) that had arrived into the fleet from the East Herts operation in November 2005 and would be one of only four Wright Crusader-bodied low-floor Darts operated in the fleet all at Stevenage depot.

Seven Dart SLF with Alexander/Transbus bodies were the newest vehicles involved in the Sovereign purchase. 3806 (KC03 PGE) was one of four new in the summer of 2003. The other trio were only three months old at time of transfer.

Around fifty vehicles were acquired in December 2000, along with the operations at High Wycombe, from Oxford Bus, which included nineteen Dennis Darts. They were transferred in with Wright, Marshall or Plaxton bodies as seen on 3822 (N522 MJO) still in its home town in 2008.

Exchanges of vehicles between Arriva fleets are commonplace. Alexander Dennis E300 3580 (KX09 GZE) was one such example, arriving at High Wycombe from Kent Thameside in June 2023, where it was the sole example of the type operated. Taken in July 2024, this would be my final Arriva photo in the town with the garage closing just a couple of weeks later.

The summer of 2009 saw a batch of twenty Alexander Dennis E300s, 3550–69, join the fleet, principally for the 300/1 route linking Stevenage with Hemel Hempstead, with the bulk of the batch allocated to Stevenage, and the last three to the latter. 3554 (KX09 GYD) is seen in 2015 leaving Stevenage bus station for Hemel Hempstead, and showing the route branding.

Similar 3568 (KX09GYV) was new to Hemel Hempstead, and is seen here at Watford Junction in the spring of 2023. All of the batch were transferred with the Hertfordshire Garages to Arriva Kent Thameside in May 2016, but retained the same fleet numbers.

Above and below: The buying policy had seen few Alexander Dennis Enviros new to the fleet, but for 2017 a total of thirty-one of the E20D model arrived, split between High Wycombe, Luton and Milton Keynes. The High Wycombe batch were moved to the Midlands fleet within a year or so of arriving. The Luton batch have mostly remained in the town and could be found over a wide variety of routes. 3113 (YX17 NMV) is seen in St Albans making its way back from Watford on what was formerly a London Country route, while 3130 (YX17 NNF) is seen in Luton having completed the same route. These were the first new vehicles to the fleet in the revised Arriva livery. With the arrival of new buses to Luton in 2025, their allocation would be cascaded to Merseyside.

The Milton Keynes share of the Alexander Dennis E20D delivery were 3119–28. Seen here at the shopping centre, 3119 (YX17 NPA) shows the Sapphire version of the 2017 livery applied to these ten vehicles for use on the busy 5/6 routes that runs between Wolverton, Central MK and Bletchley. This vehicle and 3120 would be cascaded to Midlands in 2020.

High Wycombe received a cascade of five MCV-bodied MAN 14.220 single deckers from Telling Golden Miller in early 2013, numbered 3741–5. A further two shorter 12.220 models would follow about a year later. 3744 (AE56 MBU) is seen on a route that is now run by Carousel a couple of years after arriving, while 3747 (AE56 MDV), one of the shorter examples, lays over. Five of the batch would later be converted to trainers.

Seen departing Luton Airport at the start of its trip back to Watford is Citaro 3912 (BV58 MLF), one of a batch of fourteen that were delivered during 2008 with eight for Watford that had been new in September, followed by six for Aylesbury a couple of months later.

High Wycombe based Citaro 3013 (BJ12 YPY) arrives into Central Reading in 2019 on the hourly 850 service from its home town, alongside the 800 on a similar headway but a slightly different route. A thirty-minute frequency was given to most parts of the route.

Looking like it has been recently fitted with a few new panels, 3032 (BD12 DHK) is seen at High Wycombe on a local service in February 2022. They were often the first choice on the Reading services.

Citaro 3016 (BD12 DHY) is seen on a bright February afternoon in Henley in 2018, complete with route branding for the 800 and 850 routes on its Max livery. Once withdrawn from passenger service in 2024 many of these Citaros would be converted to trainers across various Arriva fleets.

Early February 2022 sees a recently arrived Citaro reversing off stand at High Wycombe. 3025 (BD12 DHN) was one of five of the type cascaded from the recently closed Kent & Surrey garage at Guildford. Citaro operation would end when Aylesbury and High Wycombe closed in July 2024.

Arriva sourced a batch of Citaros in early 2012, many of which were initially used as games transport for the London Olympics. 3031 (BD12 DHJ) is seen working a 280 to Thame in May 2023. The route would be renumbered X7 in early 2024, with the full route to Aylesbury numbered X8 until the route ceased a few months later.

Twenty-four East Lancs-bodied Scania L113CRL with East Lancs European forty-nine-seat bodywork entered service in late 1995, split between Luton for the 31 and Hemel Hempstead and Aylesbury for the 500 routes. They were new in Luton & Districts blue and yellow livery. 3155 (N705 EUR) was one of the batch at Hemel Hempstead, but by late 2010 was an Aylesbury vehicle when seen in West Street, Dunstable, heading back home across the Chilterns.

Four additional similar vehicles arrived in mid-1996 and were put to work initially on the busy 31 route between Luton and Dunstable. 3168 (N29 KGS) is seen in Leighton Buzzard on a 70 to Luton via Dunstable.

Following on in late 1997 from the East Lancs batch were fourteen Scanias with Northern Counties Paladin bodywork split between Luton, 3191–5, and Stevenage, 3196–9/201–5. These were some of the first deliveries numbered into the new four-digit system introduced earlier in the year. 3197 (R197 RBM) is seen at the end of a working from Luton in 2008.

Late 2005 would see a batch of nineteen Scania L94UB with Wrightbus Solar forty-four-seat bodywork arrive at Luton for use on the 27 and 38 routes, the latter displacing Tridents. 3605 (KE55 CTO) is seen in 2010 very much in its original guise in Luton.

The opening of the Luton–Dunstable Busway in 2013 allowed for the speeding up of services to Leighton Buzzard. 3603 (KE55 FBY) was one of several of the batch that was fitted with guidewheels and rebranded for the then F70, which was also extended to Milton Keynes.

Intended for Luton when delivered in 2009, Scania N94UB/Wright Solar 3640/1 (KX59 ACJ/O) entered service at Milton Keynes instead, where they remained until transfer to Aylesbury in early 2021. Shortly after 3640 is seen leaving Aston Clinton for the final few miles back to Aylesbury.

A trio of Scania K230UB/Wright were cascaded from Arriva Midlands to Luton in the spring of 2022. 3515 (YR59 NNV) is seen in early 2023 at Luton Interchange, with a long queue forming opposite for the next Green Line 757 to London. This was on one of many rail strikes in that period.

Scania Omnicity bodywork is carried by 3578 (YN55 RCF), which arrived in the fleet in 2020. This was one of a pair of CN94UBs that were short-term loans from Midlands during Covid. It is seen at Milton Keynes Station Square in front of where the new Unity Place now stands.

Above and below: Arriva had taken several new DAF SB220s with Plaxton Prestige thirty-nine-seat bodywork in 1999 that were fuelled by LPG, with large roof-mounted tanks. Within a couple of years cascades placed the fleet at Watford garage, where they were converted to diesel power, which included removal of the roof-mounted tanks. Both 3269 (T493 KGB), seen in Watford, and 3278 (T492 KGB), in Luton, had been new to the now sold Arriva Scotland fleet, while others had been new to the North Wales operation.

Another similar gas bus transferred into Watford was 4428 (S428 MCC), which arrived in early 2004 from Arriva North West, being converted to diesel power the following year. It would be withdrawn after an accident in late 2014 and sold locally for scrap.

Watford received two 9.8-metre DAF SB120 Wright Cadets, 4514/5, in early 2002 for use on the W9 to Borehamwood. 4515 (KE51 PVJ) here turns into Watford Junction station stops.

Above and below: Two batches of DAF SB220s arrived into the fleet with 3401–6 at Watford in late 2007, as shown by 3403 (YJ57 BWC). They were bodied with Plaxton Prestige bodywork. These were followed in mid-2009 by 3407–12 at Stevenage with Wrightbus Pulsar bodywork. 3408 (KX09 KDK) is seen in Danestrete almost outside where the former London Country Garage once stood. All twelve vehicles would later pass to Arriva Kent Thameside with the Hertfordshire services.

Alongside its bus operations side Arriva operated as a dealer of new and second-hand vehicles, including a DAF franchise in the UK. What would later become 3812 (YJ58 FFA), a DAF SB200 with Plaxton bodywork, had seen service with Arriva both in the UK and on loan to the short-lived Malta operation where it ran as BUS309, seen here back in the UK as an Aylesbury vehicle in 2023. Quite surprisingly it retained an all-over white livery.

One of three Wrightbus Cadets on 9.4-metre DAF SB120 chassis was 3701 (KE55 CKU) that was acquired for the High Wycombe Park and Ride service in August 2005, which served a location just off the M40 to the south of the town. It was also served by Oxford Bus Airline services to Heathrow and Gatwick.

Just arrived outside Aylesbury railway station is 3731 (YJ57 BRV), a DAF SB200 Wrightbus Pulsar in July 2024 that had arrived from Arriva Midlands in 2021, by which time Aylesbury had just three routes remaining: the X5 to Hemel Hempstead, the X9 to High Wycombe and the X7 to Oxford. 3741 would soon be making its final journey to the breakers yard.

To help remove older rolling stock a batch of twenty-six DAF SB220s with Wrightbus Pulsar 2 bodywork arrived from Arriva Merseyside in 2014/5. They were split between Stevenage and Milton Keynes garages. 3876 (MX13 AMO) is seen leaving Aylesbury for the trip back home in 2023 shortly after MK took over the service from Aylesbury garage.

The summer of 2016 saw the arrival of a trio of VDL SB200 with Wright B44F bodies to Aylesbury from Arriva Midlands. They were only a couple of years old at the time, and were frequent performers on the 280 group of services to Oxford, as seen here in August 2017 as 3797 (FL63 DWX) commences an X8 service to Thame.

Purchased new by Arriva's dealing business in 2011 was this VDL 180 with MCV Evolution body. It arrived with the company in early 2020 in white and initially running unnumbered before becoming 2790 (YJ60 GGO) and allocated to High Wycombe until closure.

Above and below: Although the fleet would later lean towards the Dennis Dart for its midibus requirements during 1994, a total of thirty-two Volvo B6 with Northern Counties bodies were split between most depots, except Stevenage and Aylesbury. Ironically in 2017 an almost identical amount of AD E20Ds would arrive with similar fleet numbers. 3127 (M727 OMJ) was new to High Wycombe where it spent its entire life until withdrawn in 2010. 3135 (M715 OMJ) spent its entire career at Luton.

Above and below: A total of eight Volvo B10BLE with Wright Renown bodies were purchased in late 1999 for the busy 31 route between Luton and Dunstable. 3263 (V263 HBH) still carries the initial style livery carried by the batch in this 2011 shot, although they carried more route branding, and 3265 (V265 HBH) shows the later style of Arriva livery applied.

3300 (R524 TWR) was one of seventeen Volvo B10BLE/Wright Renowns acquired from Sovereign with the remainder of the Stevenage operations in January 2005. Originally new to Keighley & District, they would still be allocated to Stevenage when operations were transferred to Arriva Kent Thameside in 2016.

New to Stagecoach Ribble was Alexander PS-bodied Volvo B10M 3330 (M234 TBV) that had been included in the sale of the East Lancashire operation to Blazefield in 2001, then finding its way to the Sovereign fleet along with two others. These were to be the only examples of this combination to operate in the fleet. By 2008 all three were based at High Wycombe.

3299 (R608 CNM) was one of seven similar Wright Crusader-bodied Volvo B6LEs that also arrived with the Sovereign purchase in 2005, which saw the company gain outright control of services in Stevenage Town.

Six Volvo B10BLE with Alexander ALX300 bodies were purchased new in May 2000, split equally between Hitchin and Hemel Hempstead. 3457 (W457 XKX), by then Stevenage based, arrives in St Albans in 2008 with a card showing its working on route 300.

3890 (LF02 PVA) received much publicity when new, as it was hailed the 'Bus of the Future' by Arriva. Based on a Volvo B7L chassis, the Wright bodywork seated only thirty-five. With its unique configuration, ten years after its launch it is seen in Stevenage working a town route at the now closed bus station.

Complete with route branding for the Busway routes A/Z, 3896 (KX11 PZZ), one of a batch of seven Volvo B7RLEs with Wright Eclipse 2 bodywork that arrived a couple of years before the Busway opened, is seen in Church Street, Dunstable, in 2016 having just left the Busway to head into the town centre and onward to Leighton Buzzard.

A slight variation of the Arriva livery was applied to 3962 (LT63 UNF) in 2022 as a tribute to the late Rob Figgins, an avid Luton Town Football Club fan. Lettering at roof level is also carried for the Keech Cottage Hospice in the town, and an explanation was carried on the plaque below the cab window.

The Luton & Dunstable Busway opened in September 2013, and slashed the journey time between the two towns, 3956 (KX12 GZT) was one of a batch of Volvo B7RLEs to carry a split livery promoting the Busway A and Green Line 757 routes, which connected at Luton Interchange on the site of the former Luton Bute Street railway station.

Transferred down from Arriva Midlands North in early 2021 were a batch of Volvo B7RLE Wright Eclipse Urbans. 3929 (KE07 EVY) is seen in 2021 as building work on Unity Place continues in the background. A twist of fate saw this become the second vehicle with the same fleet number lost to fire damage in early 2025.

An unusual cascade from Southend arrived in late 2023, in the shape of Volvo B7RLE Wright Eclipse Urban 3906 (GN07 AVC), which had carried a former Southend Transport livery at its former home city. It's seen here on the busy 5/6 route almost twelve months later.

Just before Christmas 2021 a batch of fourteen new Volvo B8RLE with MCV Evora bodies arrived at Luton. They were a mixture of 10.8-metre, as here, and 12-metre vehicles. 3977 (LF71 DLZ) is seen when only a few days old alongside Trident 5427 (W427 XKX), which had been new to Luton in 2000 and was in the twilight of its career. With the arrival of the new eVoRas in 2025 the 10.8-metre examples including 3977 were cascaded to Arriva Merseyside.

The opening of the Busway in 2013 was the start of speeding up some other services. The long-established routes to Leighton Buzzard were incorporated into the Busway family of routes and extended to Milton Keynes, with two buses an hour. Luton's 3971 (LF71 DLN) is seen arriving at Leighton Buzzard on its way back in 2023. The route was later extended at the southern end to serve the airport.

Above and below: Spring 2025 saw thirty new vehicles purchased for the Luton–Dunstable Busway. Numbered 3201–30, they were all similar Volvo B8RLE with MCV eVoRa bodies seating forty-three. Route revisions in June saw two new services introduced to serve new developments north of the Busway, while the A–Z ran opposite loops round on the key Airport–Luton–Dunstable–Houghton Regis–Luton–Airport route, with parts of the Busway having a daytime frequency of about every four minutes. 3215 (BU25 ZBP) is seen heading out of Luton towards Dunstable with a Milton Keynes service, while 3201 (BU25 YZT) arrives back at Interchange heading towards the airport.

The following section covers the acquisition of MK Metro until its transfer to the main licence in 2013. The operator had taken their first Solos in early 1999 with a batch numbered 1–4 (S401–4 ERP). The 8.5-metre length seated thirty-one, a slight increase over the previous Mercedes Minibuses that were purchased new. S401 ERP, now numbered 2431, would move to the Arriva East Herts and Essex fleet in June 2011.

By the end of 2000 a total of eighteen new Solos had been taken by MK Metro, as well as a former Optare demonstrator. All had been standardised on the 8.5-metre option with thirty-one seats, including 2436 (X417 BBD), but further arrivals would see some 10.2-metre examples with thirty-seven seats.

More Solos would arrive into Milton Keynes after purchase by Arriva to help update the fleet. 2451 (YJ08 XDK), a M950 with thirty-three seats, was new in 2008, part of a batch of sixteen Solos to arrive between then and 2010.

Along with small batches of new single deckers, MK Metro had used the second-hand market to pick up vehicles. R514 SJM was part of a batch that arrived from Connex in 2003, and like others of the batch it would be reregistered to disguise its age, becoming HDZ 2604, with fleet number 3524 in the Arriva series replacing its former number of 84.

Delivered new to MK Metro in October 2001 was 51 (HX51 LSO), a Caetano Compass-bodied Dennis Dart SLF. It would later become 3526 in the Arriva series, and carry in-house advertising for driver recruitment.

More arrivals from Connex in 2004 included 3528 (T410 LGP), a Caetano Compass-bodied Dennis Dart SLF that again adopted a new identity when reregistered NDZ 7935 before entry to service. The Arriva livery was applied in early 2009 as the Milton Keynes allocation adopted the parent company's livery.

Late 2006 had seen the arrival of two Optare Excel L1150 into the fleet at Milton Keynes, from Ogden of St Helens. These were to remain unique in the fleet numbered 42/3 (V392/3 KVY), later becoming 3002/3 in the Arriva numbering. The former is seen passing the former central bus station. Both would later move across to Hemel Hempstead before retirement.

Showing one of many liveries operated in the then new town by MK Metro is Caetano Compass-bodied Dart NDZ 7921, again a second-hand purchase from Connex. Then numbered 57, it would later be numbered 3532 and gain Arriva livery in 2010.

Transferred into Milton Keynes at the start of 2012 was 3512 (KE51 PUX). By then already ten years old, the twenty-six-seat DAF SB120 Wright Cadet would serve for another five years. It's seen here outside the shopping centre in 2015.

Cascaded into Milton Keynes from Kent in late 2017 was 3539 (LF52 UOB), which had started life with Arriva London North as DWL50 and configured as B30D. When its London days were over the centre doors were removed for its provincial life. It's seen here on Midsummer Boulevard in early 2018.

New to Wright of Millport in October 2002 was YG52 CMU, a thirty-nine-seat DAF SB120 Wright Cadet 2 acquired in early 2004 for use in Milton Keynes, later becoming an advert for use of public transport in the new town with fleet number 3731.

Eight Scania L94UB with forty-three-seat Wrightbus Solar bodywork were purchased new in two batches of two, then six vehicles in 2005/6, with the batch numbered 81–8, later becoming 3621–8 in the Arriva series. 3623 (YN06 JXK) of the second batch shows its route branding for the busy trunk route 5 in this 2008 image.

Above and below: Five high-spec Mercedes Benz Citaros were acquired for use on route 300 Magna Park–Kingston–Coachway–Shopping Centre–Station, which featured better seating including 2 +1 configuration in the forward section. 3926 (BG59 FCV) is seen firstly at MK Coachway on its intended service, then seven years later in High Wycombe about to depart for Reading.

Above and below: The 2009 intake for Milton Keynes consisted of nine Alexander Dennis E300s route branded for either the 4 or the 5, which ran north to south across Milton Keynes. 3570 (KX09 GYY) is seen outside of Milton Keynes Central station, while 3577 (KX09 GXW) is seen across Station Square with the former bus station as a backdrop. Perhaps it was not the correct decision to build the two about 200 metres apart and the later decision to relocate the bus stops to the front of the station has paid off.

Cascades from London brought a batch of five-year-old DAF SB3000 with Van Hool bodies into Hemel in 1998 for use on the Green Line 758. 4057 (M947 LYR) is seen in early 2009 at the now closed Hemel Hempstead bus station with a mid-morning working to Victoria.

The latter part of 1997 saw ten Plaxton Prima-bodied DAF SB300s purchased for the Green Line 757 based at Luton. After the arrival of the Van Hools in 2008 they were transferred onto other routes including, as seen here in 2010, the 758 route, with 4047 (R447 SKX) at Victoria.

More new rolling stock for the 757 appeared in 2000, partly due to the additional low-cost airlines using the town's airport. 4362 (W362 XKX), being one of the ten DAF SB3000 Plaxton Primas to arrive, is seen here passing what was the old garage in the town that was redeveloped as a Matalan store in 2002.

One of the 1997 batch of DAF/Plaxtons was painted up in EasyBus colours in 2007 as part of a joint ticketing agreement between both parties and Terravision, with all three names on the first nearside window. 4054 (R454 SKX) would be another coach to pass to the training department during early 2009, before sale out of the fleet in late 2011.

Stevenage depot also operated a Green Line route into central London, via Hatfield, on which 4066 (YJ55 WSZ), a DAF SB4000 with Van Hool Alizee fifty-five-seat coachwork, is seen leaving Victoria. New in 2005, the batch of five were fitted with a wheelchair lift, hence the double looking door. They spent the first four years of their lives at Luton on the 757. The 797 route would later pass to Uno before its ultimate demise.

Rounding Hyde Park Corner 4076 (YJ05 PVT) is just a matter of minutes from its Victoria destination. The Van Hool Alizee-bodied DAF SB4000 was one of a batch of similar vehicles that had been cascaded off National Express work onto the Green Line route.

The demand for larger vehicles on the 757 prompted the purchase in the winter of 2008/9 of twelve Van Hool T917s with an impressive sixty-three seats for the route. 4378 (YJ58 FJY) is seen in early 2017 exiting the airport on its way towards the town's interchange and journey's end.

Following on from the batch of twelve Van Hool T917s was a trio that arrived a few weeks later painted for easyBus.co.uk but used on the 757. 4385 (YJ58 FFV) loads at the airport in 2010 for Victoria, with another of the batch behind. Redevelopment at the airport since has seen the bus station relocated.

4374 (YJ58 FJP) is seen at Victoria in July 2013, with intending passengers waiting to board. This adaption of the livery was carried on most of the type from 2011, with other partners again listed on the window that now include Wizz and National Express. The partnership with the latter and the airport would soon change.

Four Volvo B9Rs with Caetano bodywork including 4101 (FJ60 HYH) were cascaded from TGM in late 2014 for use on the 757. Initially new for National Express work, they were fitted with toilets unlike other vehicles used on the 757. All were withdrawn in late 2017.

While under the control of Arriva Kent Thameside, Hemel Hempstead had received four Van Hool TX17 fifty-nine-seat coaches for the 758. In September 2019 control of the route passed to Luton along with the four vehicles, but their stay was only a few months as they were not DDA compliant and were dispatched to a dealer in January 2020. Seen here attending Showbus 2017 is 9003 (YJ66 FHY).

Mercedes Benz Tourismo BJ16 KYW was loaned in from Evobus in early 2017 as a demonstrator. It's seen here at Hyde Park Corner later in the year heading back to Luton with just a 757 to identify it from other coaches in London.

Following on from the loan a batch of thirteen Tourismos arrived in the fleet during the summer of 2017 for the 757 route. 7012 (BP17 URW) heads for London via the airport from interchange with the single fare prominently displayed.

Arriva had taken delivery of sixteen Tourismos in early 2020 for a planned new service between Stanstead Airport and Central London, which, due to Covid, was never operated. All sixteen of the batch were placed in service during the second half of the year in Luton, releasing the 2018 examples back to the leasing companies. 7211 (BV20 HR0) stands at Milton Keynes Central while on rail replacement.

Late 2019 saw the arrival of six new Temsa Safari coaches for the 758, numbered 7100–5, which was now running out of Luton. All six remained in an anonymous all-over white livery during their stay. Initially put in the reserve fleet during Covid, they were then loaned to Kent & Thameside for contract work later in the year. Several returned to Luton in early 2021 but were moved on again after a few months. 7101 (YJ69 AAU) passes Luton station during its first stint with the fleet.

The summer of 2024 would see three of the Temsa Safaris return to The Shires use, for a new X1 limited stop service between Milton Keynes and Luton, running via the A5 and Dunstable, but it would not use the Busway. Operated by Milton Keynes, the hourly service would require all three vehicles but with no Sunday service. 7101 (YJ69 AAU) shows the branding adopted for the service. Revisions in September 2025 saw Luton taking over running the route with a trio of Tourismos and the Temsas moved on.

Above and below: While the company's core business is service work local to its bases, for a short period some National Express contracts were obtained, and worked by Milton Keynes, with coaches overnighting at various locations, including other Arriva garages. Seen passing through are 0422 (FJ09 DXO) at Luton and 4102 (FJ07 TKE) at the temporary MK Coachway. Both are Scania K340s with Caetano Levante bodywork.

Above and below: Preserved locally are two former vehicles that have served the fleet. 5111 (G281 UMJ), a Leyland Olympian with Leyland-built body, was new to the former London Country North West fleet as LR81, initially for London Contracts, while 3606 (KE55 CTK) was one of a batch of Scania L94UB/Wright Solar that had been new to Luton, where most of the batch spent their entire working lives.